Gandhi

Nigel Hunter

Illustrations by Richard Hook

The Bookwright Press
New York · 1987

Great Lives

William Shakespeare
Queen Elizabeth II
Anne Frank
Martin Luther King, Jr.
Helen Keller
Ferdinand Magellan
Mother Teresa
Louis Braille
John Lennon
John F. Kennedy
Florence Nightingale
Elvis Presley
Gandhi
Captain Cook
Napoleon
Einstein

First published in the
United States in 1986 by
The Bookwright Press
387 Park Avenue South
New York, NY 10016

First published in 1986 by
Wayland (Publishers) Limited
61 Western Road, Hove
East Sussex BN3 1JD, England

ISBN 0-531-18093-X
Library of Congress Catalog Card Number: 86-70988

Phototypeset by The Bath Press, Avon
Printed in Italy by G. Canale & C.S.p.A., Turin

Contents

Memories of the Mahatma

His face is familiar to people in all parts of the world, but to the people of India, Mahatma Gandhi is part of the landscape itself. In every Indian town and village, you are likely to see his image. It could be a framed portrait in the Post Office or bank or a faded photograph displayed on the crumbling wall of a back street tea shop. It could be a brightly-colored postcard clipped to the side of a street-vendor's stall; or a full-length statue set up in the restful shade of a public park or above the hurly-burly and bustle of the crossroads.

He may be pictured at his spinning wheel, absorbed in concentration, or playing with children, laughing good naturedly. Or perhaps he is drinking tea with the Viceroy. More often, he is portrayed striding purposefully forward, leading the movement for Indian independence; for freedom, peace and friendship. Millions affectionately called him *Bapu*,

Gandhi with his granddaughters in New Delhi.

father of the nation. As a sign of respect he became known as Gandhiji and was also called "Mahatma" (great soul) by one of India's finest poets, Rabindranath Tagore.

People in every part of India remember Gandhi. In the southern town of Madurai, what was once a palace is now a museum dedicated to his memory. Outside, in reconstructed buildings, his modest *ashram* living conditions are shown. Inside, a display of words and pictures portrays the long, painful, triumphant march to freedom from British rule. Behind glass there are relics of Gandhi's life: photographs, letters, documents and books; a pair of spectacles, and a spinning wheel. In one cool and carefully-lit space lies an exhibit that bears witness to his sudden, shocking death: a quantity of simple homespun-cloth, white linen darkened by the stain of blood . . .

A Hindu family

When Mohandas Gandhi was born in 1869, the British Empire was at the peak of its power. The British had ruled India for almost three centuries. Certain parts of the country, ruled by princes who were loyal to the British, were allowed to continue as separate princely states. Mohandas' father was the *Diwan*, or Prime Minister, of Porbandar, a small princely state on India's western coast. It was an appointment that passed from father to son.

His first language was Gujarati; his family's religion was Hindu. Every day, his mother prayed in the temple. She would fast for long periods and she seemed to her youngest son to be a figure of pure saintliness. He was a shy boy, who was frightened of the dark. He was not very good at school work, but he showed a rare honesty. When a teacher once slyly suggested that he should cheat to impress the school inspector, he refused point-blank to obey.

When he was thirteen his parents arranged for him to marry. In later life, he criticized the custom of child-marriage, but at the time he readily accepted it. Mohandas' bride, Kasturbai, was also thirteen, and he soon became devoted to her. He was a very strict husband, and Kasturbai felt he restrained her too much. She was supposed to get his permission before seeing her friends, or visiting the temple. Firmly, she resisted, until he grew to accept her point of view. It was a valuable lesson to Mohandas: he learned that non-violent persuasion could convince people that they were wrong. Years later, nonviolent resistance would prove to be a powerful weapon in the struggle for social and political reform.

Gandhi's wife, Kasturbai.

Gandhi's wedding. His head is covered with traditional decorations.

Pangs of conscience

For several months at a time, Kasturbai returned to live with her parents. This was customary during the early years of a child marriage. Meanwhile, Mohandas continued to attend school.

One of his Muslim friends at this time managed to convince him that meat eating was a patriotic duty. His friend said that if only more Indians ate meat, they could become as strong as "the mighty Englishmen" seemed to be, and then one day overturn British rule in India. Mohandas had

Gandhi's secret meat-eating experiment.

always thought of himself as weak and cowardly, and meat seemed a possible cure for cowardice. But his parents believed in avoiding unnecessary killing and like many Hindus, they were vegetarians. He thought they would be "shocked to death" to know he was eating meat, so he experimented with his friend in great secrecy.

However, it proved too painful to his conscience to deceive his parents for long. After eating only five or six meat dishes, he gave up meat-eating for good.

Other boyhood offenses included stealing coins from the servants with which to buy cigarettes, and stealing a piece of gold from his brother. He only stole this to pay off a debt owed by the same brother to someone else, but he felt so ashamed that he wrote a note of confession to his father. His father forgave him and the affection between father and son was greatly deepened. It was the end of Mohandas's dishonest behavior.

Some months after this incident, his father became ill, and for weeks Mohandas nursed him. Then one night, just after he had left his father to be with Kasturbai, who was now pregnant, his father died. Added to his grief, Mohandas developed a sense of guilt at not having been present at his father's death. Shortly afterward, the baby Kasturbai had been carrying died, too. Gandhi felt these two sad events were a judgment upon him for his behavior.

Widening horizons

Right *Gandhi took dancing lessons and dressed expensively to overcome his shyness.*

Gandhi was ill at ease in Britain at first. He had very little confidence but studied English manners, dressed expensively, and took dancing lessons, trying to fit into English society as a gentleman. The English diet, including meat, was difficult for him. Then he discovered that not all British people ate meat, and he became a leading member of the Vegetarian Society of

Gandhi's family hoped that he might become a *Diwan*, like his father and grandfather before him. For this, it would be a great advantage for him to study law in England. Having given a solemn pledge to his mother not to touch wine, women or meat, he sailed from Bombay in September 1888. For nearly three years, he would be away from Kasturbai, who had just given birth to a son:

England. He began to eat cheap, nourishing meals, and became interested in simplifying his life-style. He also started to write articles for the Vegetarian Society's journal. While living in London, Gandhi first read the *Bhagavad Gita*, the greatest holy book of Hinduism. As a boy, he had known some of the Hindu stories, but had not held any particular religious beliefs. He had developed friendships with people of many different religions. This helped him to develop a respect for different religions, but he remained uncommitted to any particular faith. Both the *Bhagavad Gita*, and then the Christian *New Testament*, had a profound effect on him.

As soon as he had qualified in law, Gandhi returned home to India. At first, prospects as a lawyer were uncertain because of his nervousness in public. Then a chance came to work on a business dispute in South Africa. This changed his life.

The challenge

Soon after his arrival in South Africa, while traveling to the city of Pretoria, Gandhi was forcibly ejected from a first-class train compartment. This was simply because he was Indian and the South African whites assumed that he had no right to enjoy first-class train travel. He spent the night on the station platform, considering the humiliations that the Indians in South Africa suffered daily.

90,000 Indians lived and worked in South Africa under white British rule, often in appalling conditions, and many were treated almost as slaves. Only a few hundred Indians, who owned a large amount of land, enjoyed the right to vote in the South African government. For all the Indians, government restrictions were a way of life.

Continuing his journey to Pretoria, Gandhi faced more insults. On a stagecoach, he was again shocked that he was not allowed to take a place inside the

Gandhi is ejected from a first-class train seat because he is Indian.

coach. He was then beaten by the driver for refusing to sit on the footboard, outside the carriage.

The journey to Pretoria spurred him into action. In the face of this racial injustice, Gandhi lost his public timidity and called a meeting to discuss the Indians' situation. From this, an organization emerged through which Indians could voice their discontent. Within a short time, Gandhi was acknowledged as a leader of the South African Indian community.

Meanwhile, the legal case that had originally brought Gandhi to South Africa was successfully resolved, largely through his own contribution. His method of solving the dispute was to appeal to what he called "the better side of human nature." To Gandhi, the point was not to achieve outright victory for one side over the other, but to bring both sides together in a mutually satisfactory arrangement. Before long, he was a highly successful lawyer.

It was at this time that Gandhi developed a belief that God was "absolute truth" and that the way to reach Him was through the concept of nonviolence.

In South Africa Gandhi became a highly successful lawyer. He is pictured here outside his office.

13

Toward community

Over the next twenty years, Gandhi was to lead the Indians of South Africa in their struggle for justice and equality. He developed a form of political struggle based on nonviolent civil disobedience.

In 1894, Gandhi organized a successful petition and newspaper publicity against new anti-Indian laws. He helped to set up the Natal Indian Congress, which aimed to improve life for the Indian community through educational, social and political work. Gandhi returned to his family in India, and there he publicized the injustices in South Africa and sought support to tackle the problems. When he returned to South Africa he was brutally attacked for being a trouble-maker by a white mob. As he recovered at a friend's house, a crowd gathered menacingly outside and sang "We'll hang old Gandhi on the sour apple tree . . ." He managed to escape under the cover of night, disguised as a policeman,

magazine for Indians in South Africa. It was called *Indian Opinion,* and it became crucial to the campaign for equality. His lifestyle changed. He decided to give up all his possessions and established a community. Here, he detached himself from his normal family ties. Gandhi believed that to serve others, he must not distract himself with the burden of possessions or involvement with family and the pleasures of family life.

Left *Gandhi is attacked by a mob.*

Below *The newspaper Gandhi started.*

and said that he forgave his attackers.

During the Boer War (1899–1902) between Britain and the South African Boers, Gandhi formed and led the Indian Ambulance Corps, which worked for the British Army. Since he was demanding rights as a citizen, he felt he owed loyalty to the British Empire; and Britain awarded him a medal. After the war he visited India again, and renewed his contacts with the leaders of the country's growing nationalist movement.

On his return to South Africa in 1903 Gandhi started a

Nonviolent rebels

A new law in South Africa required all Indians over eight years old to register with the authorities, and carry a pass at all times. Failing this, they could be imprisoned, fined, or deported. Under Gandhi's leadership, the Indians resisted this new law. He called their action *satyagraha*, which means "holding to the truth." They would not cooperate with the authorities and their resistance was to be nonviolent. Courageously, they confronted prison, poverty, hunger, and violence against them, peacefully refusing to obey the law.

In 1908, Gandhi visited London to muster support. On his return to South Africa, he was imprisoned. Still wearing prison uniform, he was taken to meet General Jan Christiaan Smuts, the South African leader. Smuts promised that if the Indians registered, he would repeal the registration law. Trusting him, Gandhi called on all Indians to register. But Smuts broke his word. In protest, Gandhi led a

Gandhi made marmalade and baked bread at Tolstoy Farm.

public burning of the registration certificates. The campaign continued, with thousands of Indians inviting arrest by refusing to register.

Gandhi spent much of his time in prison reading and writing. He discovered the works of the famous Russian writer Leo Tolstoy, and, inspired by each other's ideas, they began exchanging letters. With the help of a friend, Gandhi founded a new community called *Tolstoy Farm*. The community members grew their own food, made their own clothes and built their own homes. Gandhi himself baked bread and made marmalade, and helped to teach the children.

More new laws, including one that said only Christian marriages were legal, prompted Gandhi to step up his campaigning. Again and again he was jailed, along with thousands of others. Many people were assaulted by the police, and several died. Finally, on the main issues, Smuts gave way. With this vital experience behind him, Gandhi was ready to return to India.

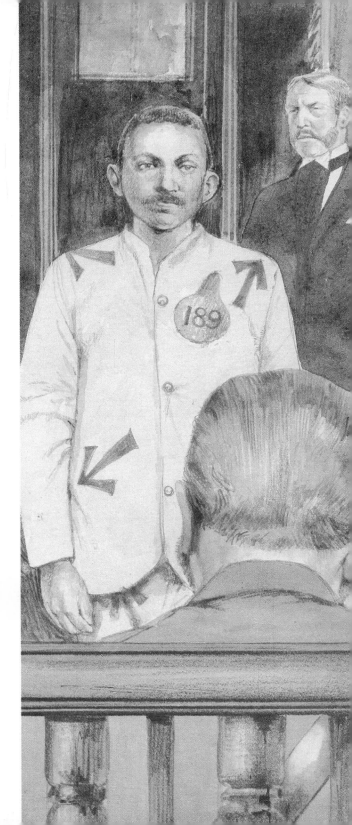

Smuts confronts the prisoner Gandhi.

An Indian future

In Bombay in 1915, Gandhi was welcomed as a hero. He no longer wore western clothing, and he chose to speak Gujarati rather than English, as English was the language of the oppressor. For a year, he toured the country, speaking on religious and social matters. He visited the community that had been started by the poet Rabindranath Tagore. Tagore shared many of Gandhi's ideals. He compared Gandhi to Buddha, because like Gandhi, he had also taught the

importance of kindness to all living creatures. Outside the city of Ahmedabad, Gandhi founded the *Satyagraha Ashram*, a community committed to non-violence and service to others.

Gandhi was determined to break down the Hindu "caste" system, which prevented the caste of Hindus who traditionally did the dirtiest work, from ever entering temples. They were called the "untouchables" because their mere touch horrified higher class Hindus. Despite opposition from Kasturbai and others who

Gandhi toured India, talking to the people.

found it hard to accept, he brought an "untouchable" family into the *Ashram* and renamed them *Harijans*, meaning "Children of God."

Gandhi successfully led the workers of the province of Bihar in a nonviolent campaign against the unjust demands of British landowners. He carried out a fast, threatening to starve himself to death unless his demands were met. His action resulted in better wages and conditions for mill workers. He also inspired farm workers who were suffering the effects of famine not to pay Government tax demands, and eventually the demands were

The poet Tagore, who shared many of Gandhi's ideals.

withdrawn. He always appealed to his opponents' sense of right and wrong. Briefly, during World War I (1914–18), he helped to recruit Indian soldiers for the British Army. This seemed at odds with his belief in nonviolence; but he hoped that service to save the Empire would earn India self-rule after the war. However, Britain passed harsh new laws preventing India from becoming a self-governing country within the Empire.

19

Turning and turning

When Gandhi heard about the new British laws, preventing Indian Home Rule, he called on all Indians to suspend business for a day of national, nonviolent protest, including fasting, prayer and public meetings. But troops in Delhi killed nine people, and when Gandhi tried to reach the city, he was arrested and turned back. News of this provoked rioting and violence in several places. It seemed to Gandhi that he had made a grave mistake. People still did not understand that *satyagraha* persuasion should be nonviolent. He punished himself by fasting for three days.

Then came the terrible massacre at Amritsar. On April 13, 1919, about 15,000 people had gathered together to demonstrate peacefully on the day of the Sikh New Year. Suddenly, soldiers of the British Army appeared, under the command of General Reginald Dyer. He gave the order to shoot, and for ten minutes the soldiers fired into the crowd, who were trapped in a square. Nearly 400 men, women and children were killed, and 11,000 wounded.

Gandhi was horrified by the brutality of the British Army in India.

Gandhi himself enjoyed spinning every day.

Gandhi was horrified by the brutality of the British Army, directed at unarmed subjects of the Empire. His loyalty to the British was completely shattered. He felt they had clearly lost all right to govern.

In 1920, Gandhi became president of the All-India Home Rule League, which sought independence from the Empire. Following this, he became the leader of the Indian National Congress. He launched a massive program of non-cooperation against the British. Cotton cloth made in Britain was boycotted and clothes made of foreign material were burned on great bonfires. To symbolize getting rid of foreign influences, hand-spinning and weaving were revived throughout the country. To Gandhi, spinning represented economic progress, national unity and independence from the Empire. He himself spun daily.

High ideals

The Indian National Congress, led by Gandhi, now called on all Indian soldiers and civilians to quit British Government service. By 1922, 30,000 people, including nearly all the Congress leaders, had been imprisoned for acts of civil disobedience. Then twenty-two policemen who had attacked the stragglers of a protest march were viciously slaughtered.

Realizing that even now the nonviolent nature of *satyagraha* was not understood, Gandhi called off the campaign, and fasted again, punishing himself for the violence he felt was his fault. He was then put on trial, accused of stirring up trouble.

In court, Gandhi spoke movingly of the people's misery under British rule and of the absurd laws. He said that perhaps in reality he was innocent, but under these laws, he was guilty, so he expected the highest penalty. The judge, although he praised Gandhi "as a man of high ideals and of a noble and even saintly life," sentenced him to six years' imprisonment.

Two years later, Gandhi was released. For three weeks he fasted in protest against the increasing conflict between Hindus and Muslims. Then he turned his attention to social reforms, touring the country by train, cart, and on foot, speaking to vast crowds. Many of his followers considered him a saint, and he was showered with gifts, which he turned into funds for the cause. He taught the importance of equality for women and for people of different classes and religions. He encouraged spinning and discouraged taking alcohol or using drugs.

In 1928 a Royal Commission arrived from Britain to review the situation in India. Since it included no Indian members, it was met by protest meetings, which were broken up by the British authorities. The new proposals would have still left the country subject to British control. Now the Indian National Congress decided it could accept nothing less than complete independence.

In court, Gandhi spoke movingly of the people's misery under British rule.

A pinch of salt

The Salt March of 1930 began a new round of nonviolent protest. Gandhi walked 322 km (200 miles) to the coast at Dandi. Thousands joined the march, watched by the world's press. On the beach after morning prayers, Gandhi picked up a lump of sea salt.

Salt was taxed; legally, only the Government could extract it from sea water. Gandhi's signal prompted people all along the coast of India to defy the law by manufacturing salt. In cities and villages, illegal salt was distributed. Following this action, about 100,000 people, including Gandhi and other Congress leaders, were imprisoned. Bravely, without violence, they faced police brutality. Many were badly beaten and some died; but eventually, the campaign succeeded, and salt manufacturing was allowed.

Later, Gandhi took part in The Round Table conference in Britain about the future of India.

Gandhi arrives at Buckingham Palace.

The Lancashire mill workers were impressed with Gandhi's sincerity and humor.

While in London he chose to stay in an East End hostel for the poor. He visited Lancashire and made friends among the mill workers, even though many were unemployed because of the Indians' boycott of British cloth. He met politicians and celebrities, and went to tea at Buckingham Palace. Everywhere, he impressed people with his sincerity and humor. As for his manner of dress at the Palace, he said, "The King was wearing enough for both of us!"

Only a week later, when he returned to India, he was imprisoned again. Before long, 30,000 others had been arrested too. In prison, Gandhi carried out a prolonged fast against the class divisions among Hindus. He was willing to starve himself to death, if the barriers were not broken down throughout the country. People valued Gandhi's life so greatly that he succeeded in changing traditions that were thousands of years old. For the first time, temples were opened to *Harijans*, and all Hindus could eat together, drink water drawn from the same wells, and even marry each other.

Gathering clouds

After his release, Gandhi turned to educational and welfare work. He toured rural India, speaking on health care, village industries and reorganization, and about land ownership and justice.

Gandhi opposed Indian involvement in World War II (1939–44), believing now that all war was wholly wrong. Leading members of the Indian Congress, including his close friend Jawaharlal Nehru, disagreed. They were willing to cooperate with the British if they could obtain reforms that would lead to self-government. But Britain would give no promise of independence.

Under Gandhi's direction, people made speeches and signed written protests against taking part in the war. Thousands, including Nehru, were imprisoned for up to a year.

In 1942 Gandhi announced a new *satyagraha* campaign aimed directly at British withdrawal

Gandhi and Nehru disagreed about Indian involvement in World War II.

There were many scenes of violence between Muslim and Hindu groups.

from India. Once again, he was imprisoned. While in prison, he fasted again, coming close to death, in protest against accusations that he had stirred up violence against the British. Kasturbai was one of 100,000 other prisoners. Her health was poor, and in 1944 she died. Feeling her loss keenly, Gandhi himself became ill, recovering only after his release a few months later. With the end of World War II, Indian independence came closer.

Gandhi had always contested religious divisions. Most Indians were either Hindus or Muslims.

In the northwest and northeast of the country, Muslims were in the majority. Their leader, Muhammad Ali Jinnah, favored the creation of a separate Muslim state there, to be called Pakistan. Congress, like Gandhi, wanted a united India. Nehru was appointed Prime Minister of a provisional Indian Government, which meant Indian rule by a Hindu for that area. Jinnah announced that the Muslim League would hold a day of action to protest. The result was horrifying violence between Muslims and Hindus, with 20,000 killed or injured.

The peacemaker

From the rural area of Bengal came reports of Muslim atrocities. Gandhi walked through the villages for four months, seeking desperately to persuade people to end the violence. But soon after, in a neighboring province, there were similar Hindu atrocities to quell.

In 1947 Lord Louis Mountbatten became the last British Viceroy of India. Reluctantly, and against Gandhi's opposition, the Indian National Congress agreed that Pakistan was to become a country in its own right, separate from India. Independence came on August 15, 1947. Gandhi was living in the poorest quarters of Calcutta, where there had been appalling bloodshed, riots and fighting between the Hindu and Muslim communities. While he succeeded in pacifying the people of Bengal, the northwest was in uproar. Millions of people were migrating across the new border separating "Muslim" Pakistan from "Hindu" India. Massacres were widespread, causing almost a million deaths. When violence

Gandhi's fast brings him near death.

The world wept at Gandhi's funeral.

broke out again in Calcutta, Gandhi undertook a fast "to death," refusing food until the northeast was peaceful. Then, in riot-torn Delhi, came his "greatest fast." Dramatically, it brought a pledge of peace among all the community leaders, and throughout India and Pakistan, the violence ceased.

Though millions revered him, and cherished his life so deeply, to some Hindu fanatics, Gandhi was an obstacle. On January 30, 1948 he was murdered—shot three times by an assassin who stepped from the crowd at a prayer meeting. His death caused worldwide shock and sorrow. To countless people, he was a modern-day saint, a teacher of humanity such as the world has rarely seen. As a champion of peace, his influence still remains.

A familiar image of Mahatma Gandhi.

Important dates

1869   Mohandas Karamchand Gandhi born in Porbandar (October 2).

1883   Marries Kasturbai Makanji.

1888–91   Becomes a law student in London

1893   Arrives in South Africa.

1896   Visits India and then returns to South Africa with Kasturbai and their sons.

1899–1900   Helps the British in the Boer War, with the Indian Ambulance Corps.

1901–02   Visits India.

1903   Begins influential journal in South Africa called *Indian Opinion*.

1904   Establishes Phoenix Farm.

1906   The *satyagraha* campaign begins.

1908   First prison sentence.

1909   He writes first book: *Hind Swaraj* or Indian Home Rule.

1910   Following correspondence with Leo Tolstoy, Tolstoy Farm established.

1913–14   Massive *satyagraha* campaign gains large measure of success.

1914   He leaves South Africa and visits Britain.

1915   Returns to India; tours the country; establishes the Satyagraha Ashram near Ahmedabad.

1919   The Amritsar Massacre.

1920   Becomes President of the All-India Home Rule League.

1922–24   He is imprisoned again.

1925–28   Tours India, speaking on social reforms. Writes his autobiography called *The Story of My Experiments with Truth*.

1930   The Salt March.

1931   The Round Table Conference, London.

1932   He is imprisoned again. He fasts against the unfair treatment of the "untouchables," the *Harijan* Hindus.

1933–39   Tours India, speaking on welfare and social issues.

1939   Start of World War II.

1942–44   Imprisoned for calling on Britain to leave India. Death of Kasturbai, February 1944.

1946–47   Widespread Hindu–Muslim troubles.

1947   Indian Independence (August 15). Creation of Pakistan.

1948   January 30: Assassination of Mahatma Gandhi.

Glossary

Ashram A community of people in India, living their lives by religious principles.

Boer White South Africans of Dutch descent.

Boycotted Refused to deal with or use.

Buddha A religious teacher who founded Buddhism, a religion that says perfection can be reached by ending greed and hatred.

Caste A term for the four inherited Hindu social classes or divisions. The "outcastes" were the "untouchable" Hindus, renamed *Harijans* by Gandhi.

Congress The representatives who meet to make state decisions.

Diwan The Prime Minister of a princely state in colonial India.

Fast Refusal to take food, often for religious or political reasons.

Home Rule Local self-government within the British Empire.

Hindu Someone who follows the beliefs of Hinduism, the religion now dominant in India.

Muslim A follower of the religion of Islam. Now dominant in Pakistan.

Satayagraha Gandhi's term for the power of truth or love, as a force to create change in the world.

Vegetarian Someone who does not eat meat or fish.

Viceroy (of India) The governor, representing the British king.

Books to read

Cheney, Glenn A. *Mohandas Gandhi.* New York: Franklin Watts, 1983.

Freitas, F. *Bapu.* Pomona, CA: Auromere, 1979.

Gandhi, Mahatma. *Mahatma Gandhi.* Edited by Ann Redpath. Mankato, MN: Creative Education, 1985.

Joshi, Uma. *Stories from Bapu's Life.* Pomona, CA: Auromere, 1979.

Rawding, F. W. *Gandhi and the Struggle for India's Independence.* Minneapolis, MN: Lerner Publications, 1982.

Shankar, R. *The Story of Gandhi.* Pomona, CA: Auromere, 1979.

Spink, Kathryn. *Gandhi.* North Pomfret, VT: David & Charles, 1984.

Index